Still more
frustration

CLAIRE BRETECHER

Still more of frustration

*TRANSLATED FROM THE FRENCH
BY ANGELA MASON AND PAT FOGARTY*

A Methuen Paperback

First published in Great Britain 1986
by Methuen London Ltd
11 New Fetter Lane, London EC4P 4EE
Copyright © 1975, 1976, 1977, 1978, 1979, 1980, 1981, 1982,
1983, 1984, 1985, 1986 Claire Bretécher
Translation copyright © 1986 Angela Mason and Pat Fogarty

Printed and bound in Great Britain
by Richard Clay (The Chaucer Press) Ltd
Bungay, Suffolk

British Library Cataloguing in Publication Data

Bretécher, Claire
 Still more frustration.
 I. Title
 741.5'944   PN6747.B/

 ISBN 0-413-14140-3

HOPE AGAINST HOPE

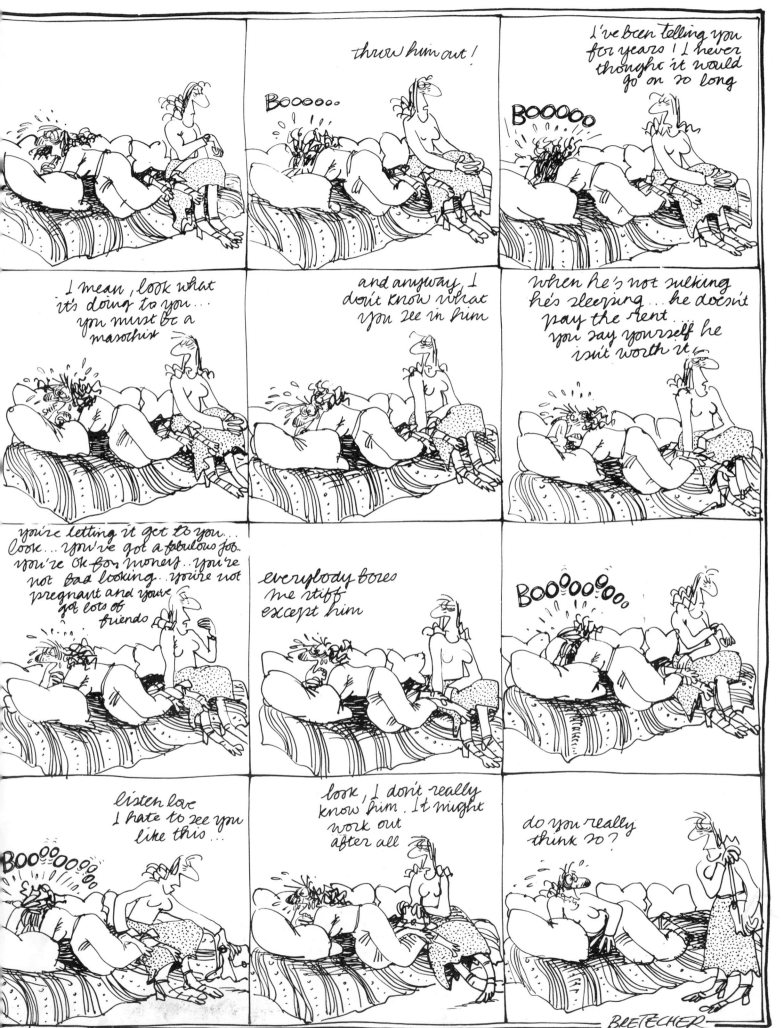

A WOMAN'S TOUCH

I just feel absolutely awful... I don't know what it is

objectively everything's ok

work's fine, Clive's absolutely adorable, the child is amazing, the au pair's perfect

But I feel drained I don't know why... I'm just in a dreadful state

maybe it's pre-menstrual

I don't know, everyone bores me, there's no point, I hate myself

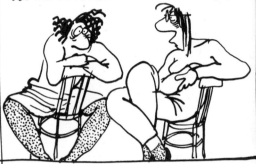

We're ok for money, we've got friends, we see people all the time. I don't understand

perhaps it's the weather

I'm not really depressed, it's more a lack of interest

perhaps your Saturn is in Scorpio

I don't know, in a week we're going to Marrakesh and I don't even feel like going

I don't understand, I just feel terrible

what about you, are you ok?

no

But I know why. I can't get social security, I can't find a job, my flat is too small, I don't have a man and I'm sick of being alone

oh don't... that's all I need

BRETECHER

PLUS ÇA CHANGE

oh do look - this spring's shock-horror article on the vexed question of Cellulite

what is it this time? lymphatic drainage? laser treatment? algae mud baths?

No, this time they're activating the sub-cutaneous fat

ah

are we being ionized?

No, they're injecting us with cortico-steroids

they must be saving the gamma rays for the September issue

once upon a time there was Dr X...

and bride-to-be Miss D, who was absolutely desperate about the size of her bottom

what husband-tobe is ever desperate about the size of his bottom?

by the 5th treatment Miss D had lost 7 inches off each thigh

a new record! I trust Dr X planted a flag on what was left

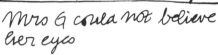

wait wait, it's fantastic, cortico-steroids don't only dissolve fat but actually improve muscle tone

the butchers! next they'll come at us with a hack-saw

listen to this: if you don't have a waist Dr X can CARVE you one, which is what he did to Mrs G

I hope he stopped when he got to the stomach

Mrs G could not believe her eyes

another giant step for science!

they're all quacks aren't they?

what do you mean? it's a serious medical article

what else is there in Harper's?

An interview with Doris Lessing

and how many inches has she lost?

they don't say

BRETÉCHER

FREELANCE

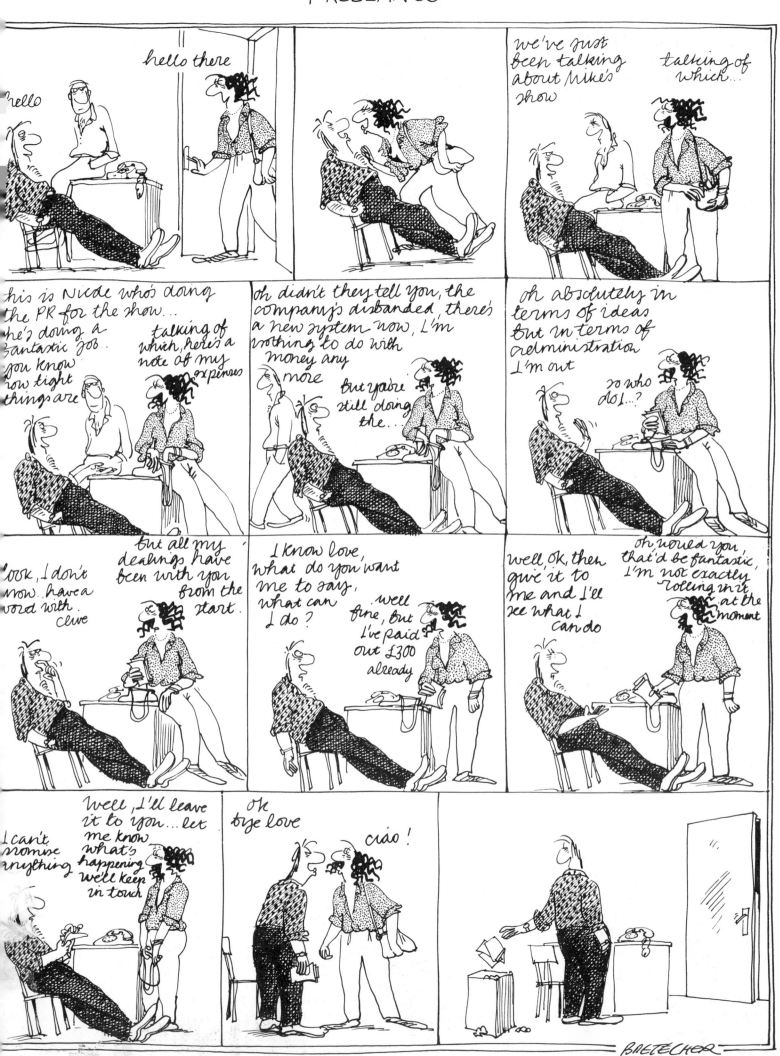

FREELANCE II

these pseudo-intellectual Islington trendies who think they own the universe ...I HATE them

they're crass, banal, loud, boring and thick.... they're just nothing... and it's all so incestuous

important things are happening and they don't even know it...they're far too busy studying their own navels

hey get paid for making a lot of noise and managing their own ego... they make me puke

Well at least they keep publishers, the press and the film industry going... that can't be bad...... you're joking!

Nothing personal but I think they just stifle creativity, they're too smug and complacent to do anything!

I'm not saying there aren't good things now and again....I mean personally I like your book a lot, even if ...its not art it works:

I think it's important to remember that most of us do a normal day's work, we're never on the box and are just as intelligent as that lot

seeing it all from the outside makes you want to kick the lot of them up the arse

on the other hand

I have to admit that we've got our own little intellectual scene going in Norwich too

BLETCHER

15

LA BOHEME

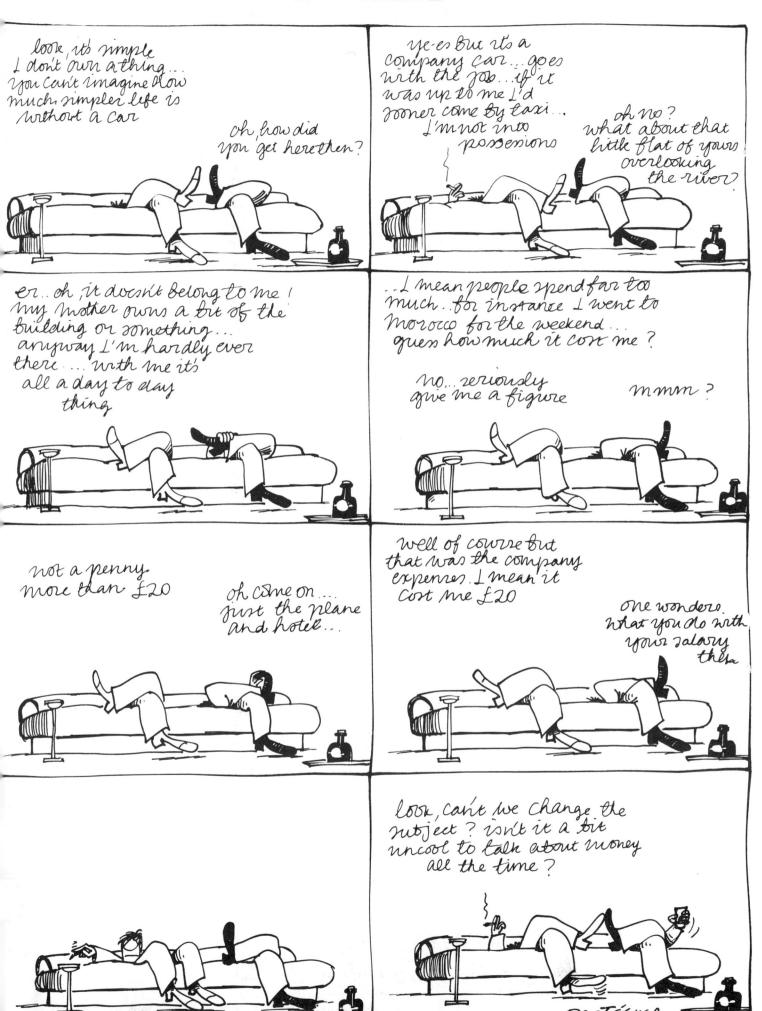

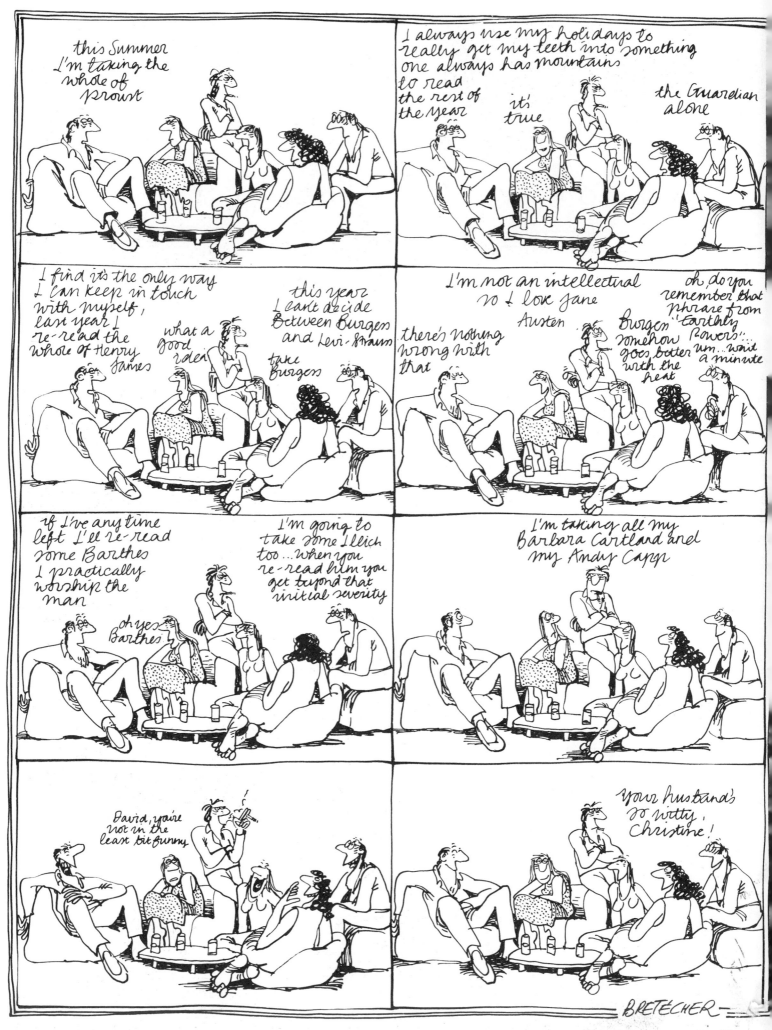

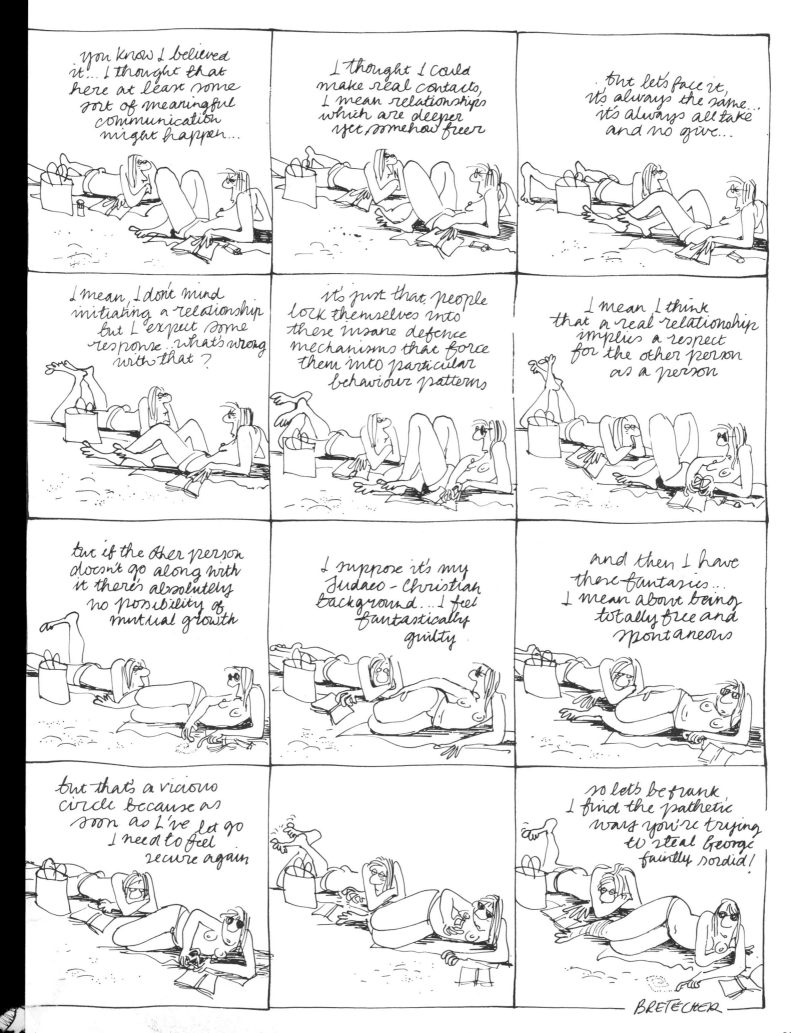

alienation

WINTER SUN

What have you been doing? Where did you get that tan? ... Oh... I've been to Florida

On a creative management course... the firm paid... but it was fantastic... all in... five star... fabulous

What sort of course was it?

Well, the first day was to do with concentration and relaxation and breathing properly...

then you have lunch.. then there's a discussion about Creativity but very free and flexible... your own VDU and earphones... then you eat.. then you relax.

the second day they flash colours on the screen and you say what they remind you of by pressing a button

for example if it reminds you of a bird you press 'B' and the computer does the rest... then you eat. by the way the food's amazing!

there's a lot going on... they invite all sorts of famous people... it's all very relaxed

you can discuss their ideas with them over dinner...

but it's not all work... there's a disco, cinema, theatre, bar, all very well done

it's all on a private estate... pool, sauna, gym, barbecue, gorgeous women

it must cost the firm a fortune... but if it's good for business, that's fine by me

although I couldn't care less right now, I can't wait to get away on holiday

BRETECHER

HOLIDAY ROMANCE

WALKABOUT

YOUR VOTE COUNTS

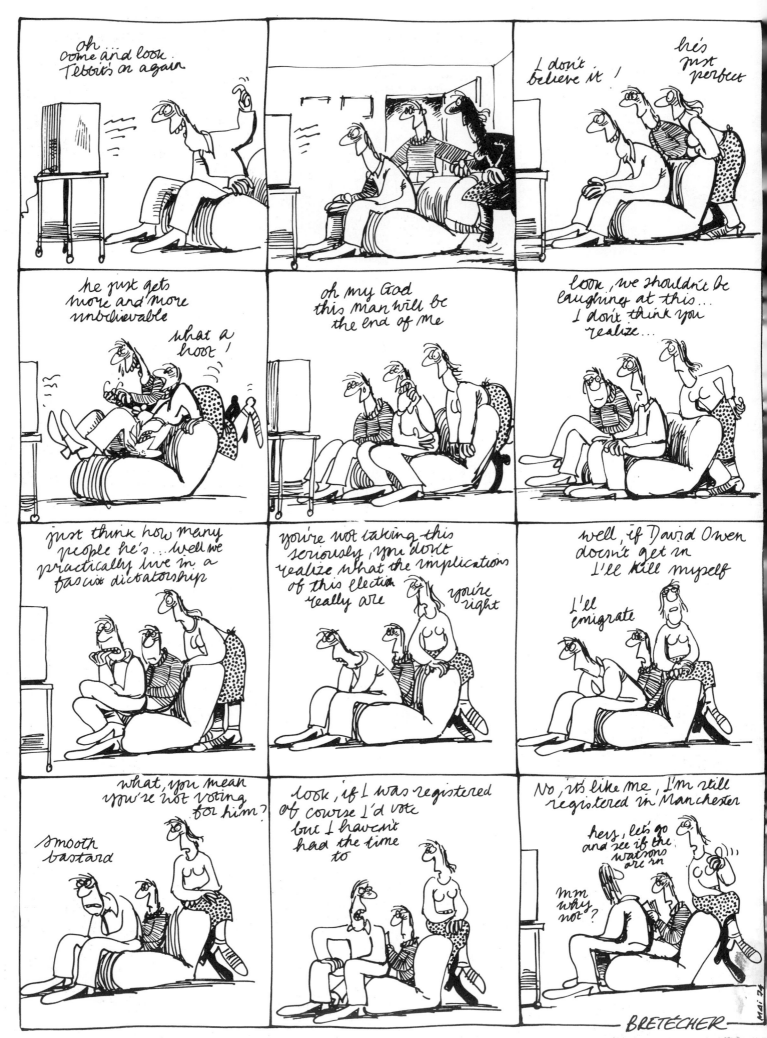

31

WARREN STREET

THE SIMPLE LIFE

last Easter when we were staying in Sophie's house in Cumbria I spent a lot of time talking to the gardener...

an amazing man - he really taught me a lot

I mean he wasn't cultured or anything and he only had a vocabulary of about two thousand words

still I didn't have any trouble relating to him.... I mean we developed a real rapport

obviously I talked to him about things that mattered to him - the soil...

...the seasons...the trees... I mean a tree is a tree is a tree...that really taught me something

the wisdom...the innocence the sheer humanity of the man was amazing

you know he was quite right... we just don't know how to live

I mean meeting him has made me understand that class barriers really don't exist

BRETÉCHER

33

GOOSEBERRY

look, I'm going to fetch Clive from the station - he's got some time off ... why don't you come too?

oh I don't want to be in the way

of course you won't be in the way silly, you're an old friend

anyway, you know quite well Clive's always pleased to see you

oh, do you think so?

I can hardly believe we're actually getting married in six months, do you realise what that means...

no, of course you don't ... you've never had a boyfriend

mind you it might happen to you too... although you don't meet a man like Clive every day... he's fantastic isn't he?

mmm....

weren't you once a little bit in love with him yourself?

me? of course not who told you that? people are fools!

anyway, I'm madly in love with him

Clive... HA HA Him? He's hardly my type... I mean even if he wasn't with you... it's unthinkable!

you're over-reacting
I was only teasing
you

I'm glad
you find it
funny

oh that reminds me
I can't come after all
I've just remembered.
there's
something
I've got to
do

what
exactly?

oh just
something

oh come on now
don't get into a state
just because I said
Clive will be glad
to see you

frankly I think I'm
on to a good thing with
him...he's intelligent
and funny and he's
never boring

and when it comes to
you-know-what he isn't
boring either ...in fact
in that department he's
absolutely incredible

after two whole months
without it you can imagine
what we'll be up to
can't you?

I'm not offending you
am I? It doesn't worry
me but I know some people
are easily shocked...
I can't imagine why

what time's
the train?

I'm just like that
about sex...I can't do
without it...it's as
simple as that

I'd better
be going

what's so important
it can't wait? are
you pre-menstrual
or angry or something?

why should
I be angry?

41

HEATWAVE

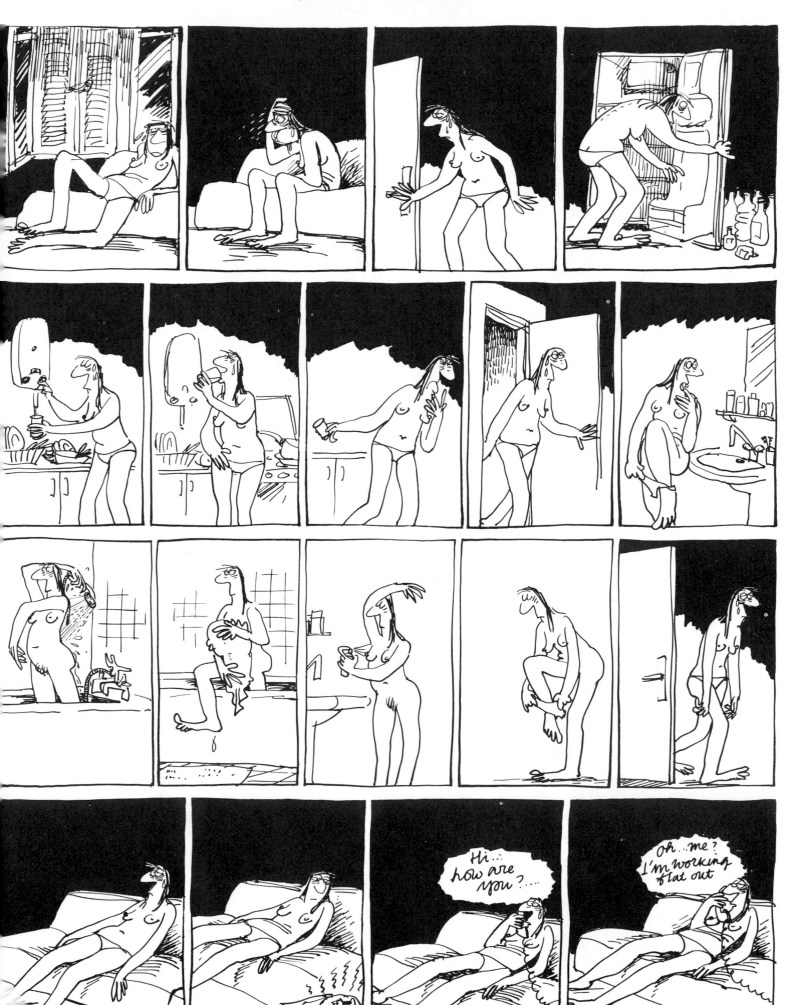

REPRESSION

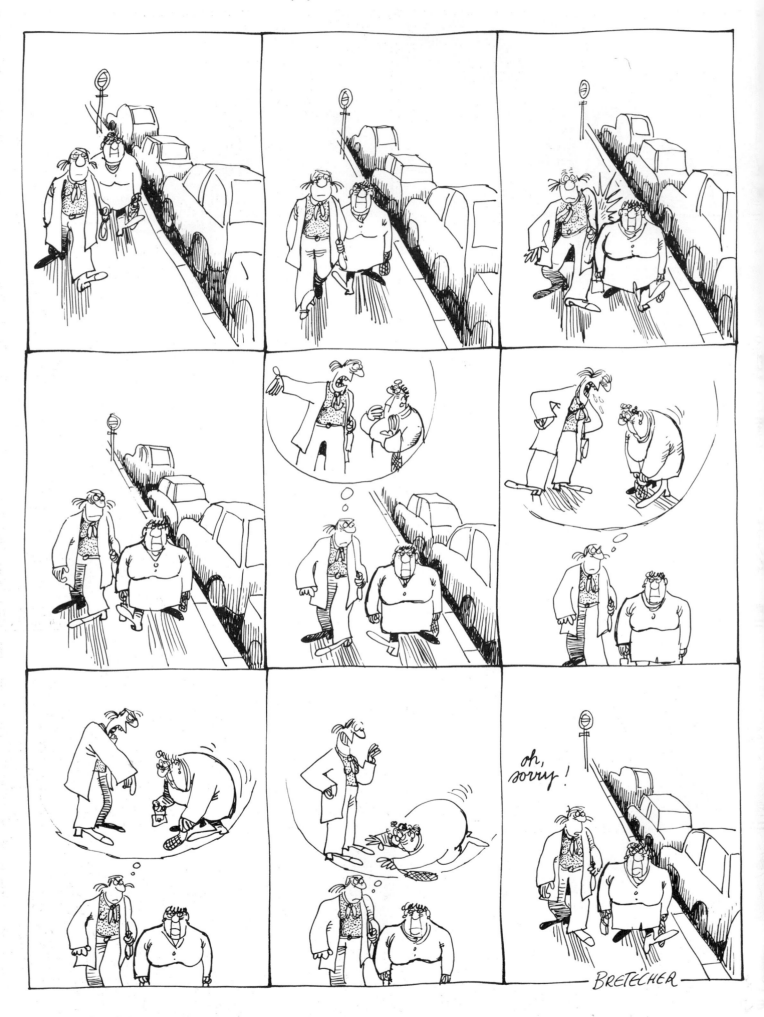

COVENT GARDEN

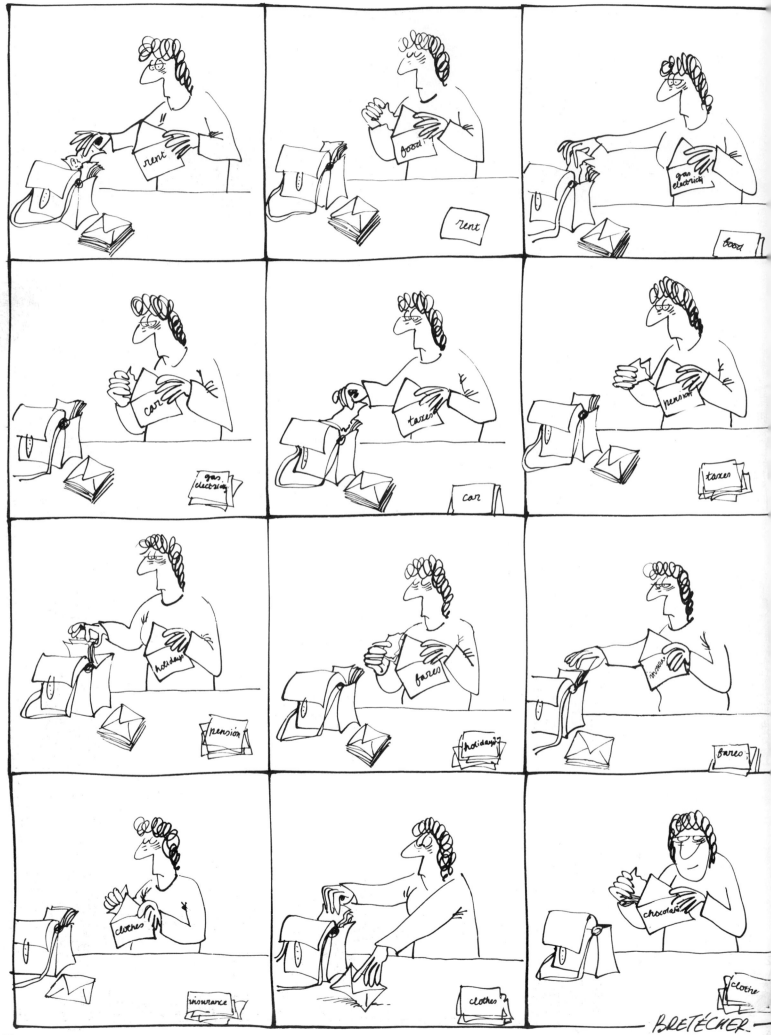

FRISÉE AUX LARDONS

47

IN THE RED

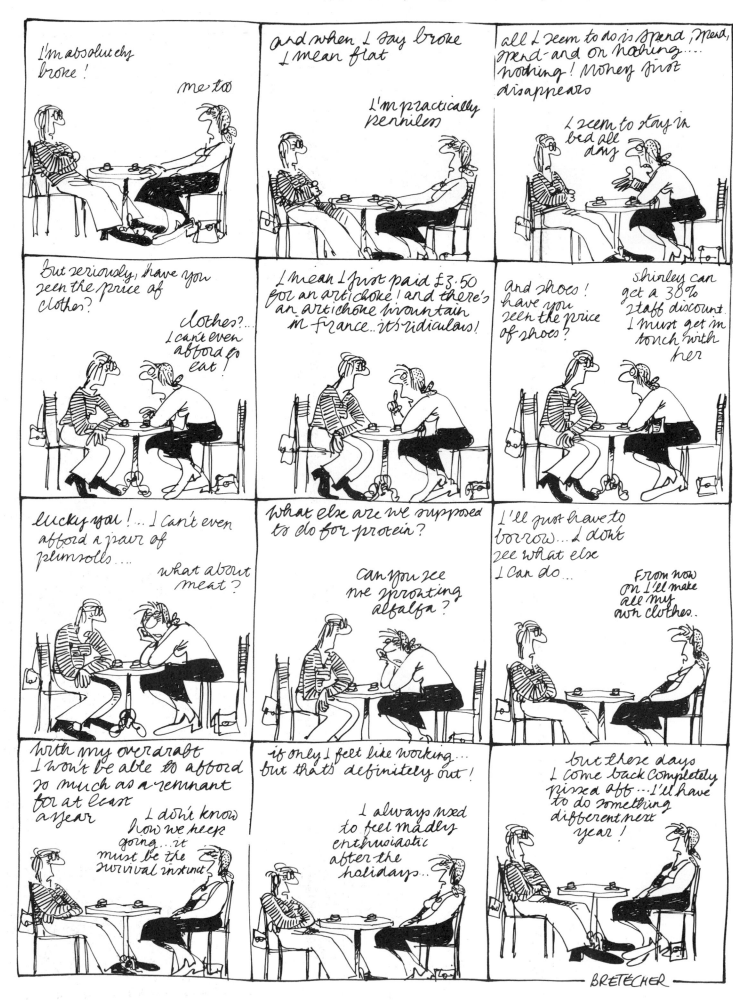

Hello Poppet, what a lovely satchel... just back from school?

oh don't

what's that funny smell, it's not him is it?

please don't

I made a big mistake getting him a proper satchel I thought it was kind of authentic... I could kick myself

so?

term hadn't even started, he put it on straight away he didn't want to take it off, he even slept in it!

so?

the next day I took him to playschool and guess what? no room and there won't be for another month!

so?

he won't be parted from that bloody satchel. I can't undress him... I can't wash him...

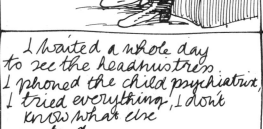

I waited a whole day to see the headmistress. I phoned the child psychiatrist, I tried everything, I don't know what else to do..

what if you gave him a good smack for once

he couldn't care less, he likes being a pain in the arse

what a lovely satchel! can I have a look at it?

I told you he doesn't want to

I'm telling you he smells

what can I do?

I don't think I can handle this

BRETECHER

FIONA

BRETECHER

51

but what is it
that interests you
in life, can you
tell me?

euaaaa!

yes I know...
you don't give a damn
about anything,
you want to work as
little as possible,
earn as much as possible
and be left alone
am I right?

boooo!

you just don't realize
that it's all a question
of politics
do you?

beuaaaa

and sex,
I suppose you never
think about that
either...

euaaaa

for you it's all
permissiveness
and you couldn't
care less

beueueu

don't talk
like that
I feel sick

to start with
I'm not interested
in permissiveness
and I'm against
abortion

I want to
get married
and have
children

you're really
mean to try
and make
Mum believe
all that
rubbish

oh, she loves it,
it gives her
something to
talk about

if she only
knew that I
couldn't care less
what I think
it would finish
her off

BRETECHER

53

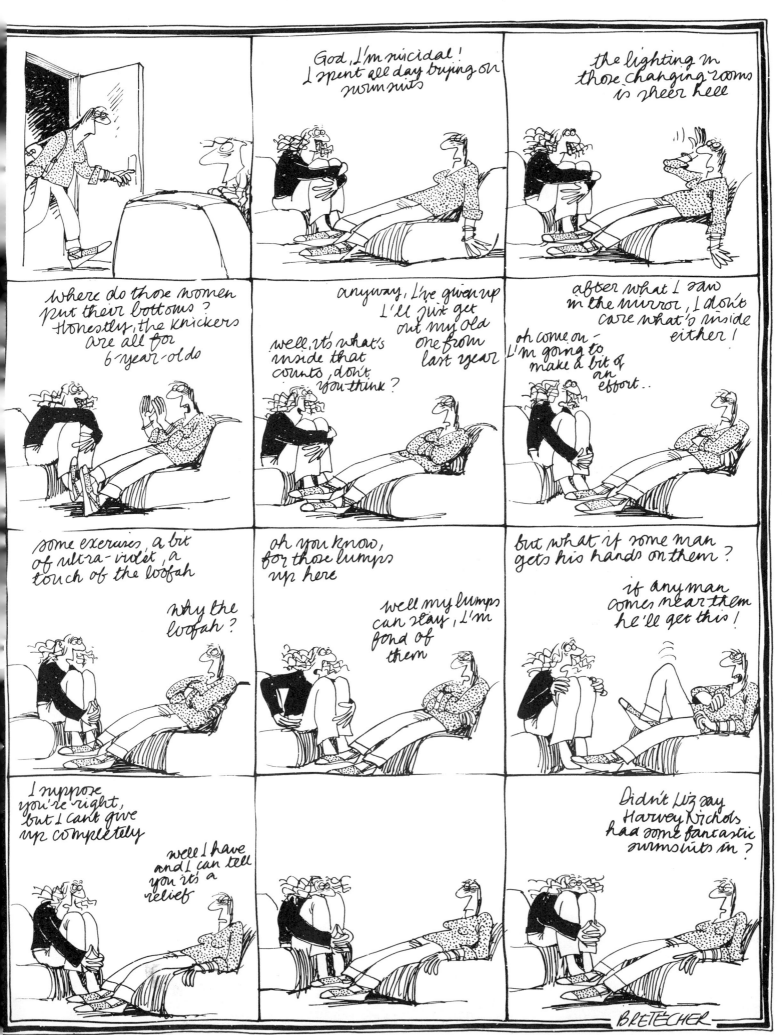

Brown Pills

BRETECHER

56

PLUMBING THE DEPTHS

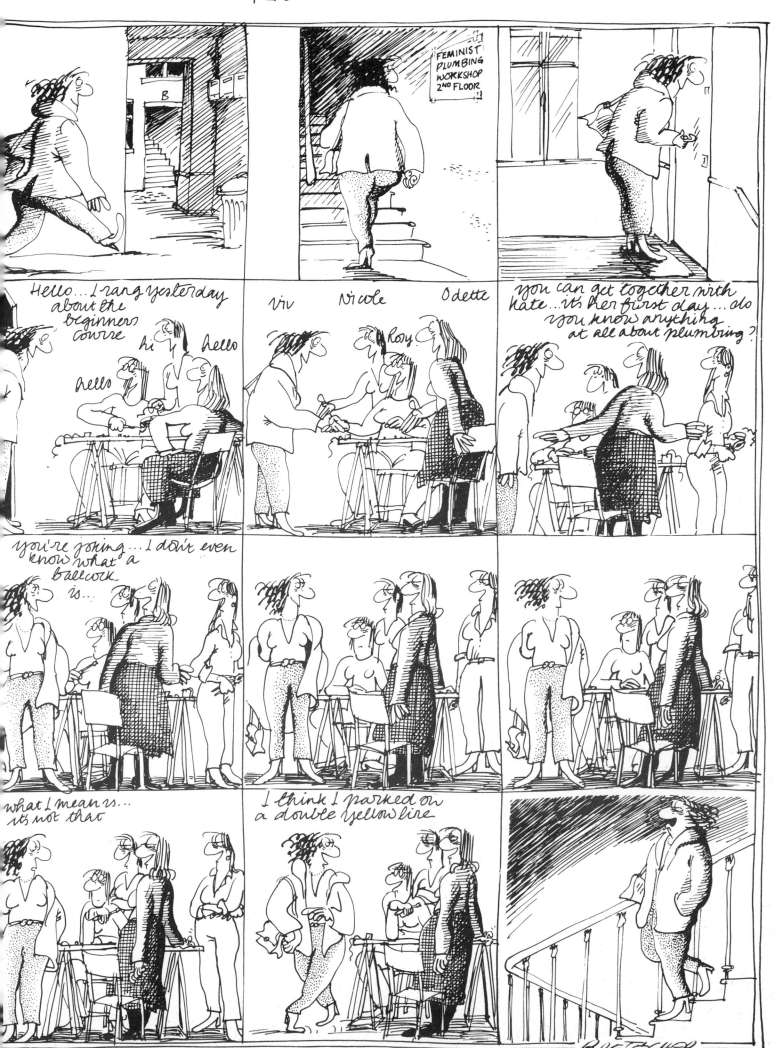

FEMINIST PLUMBING WORKSHOP 2ND FLOOR

Hello... I rang yesterday about the beginners course

hi / hello

hello

Viv   Nicole   Odette

Rosy.

you can get together with Kate... it's her first day... do you know anything at all about plumbing?

you're joking... I don't even know what a ballcock is...

what I mean is... it's not that

I think I parked on a double yellow line

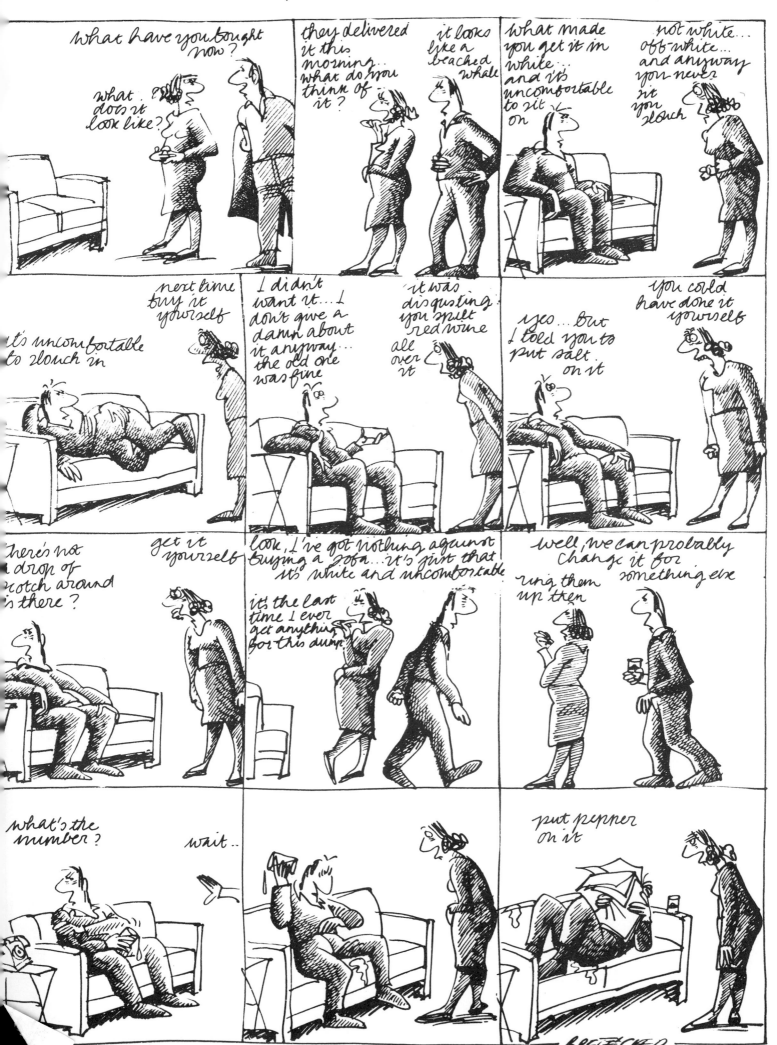

The Liberal parent

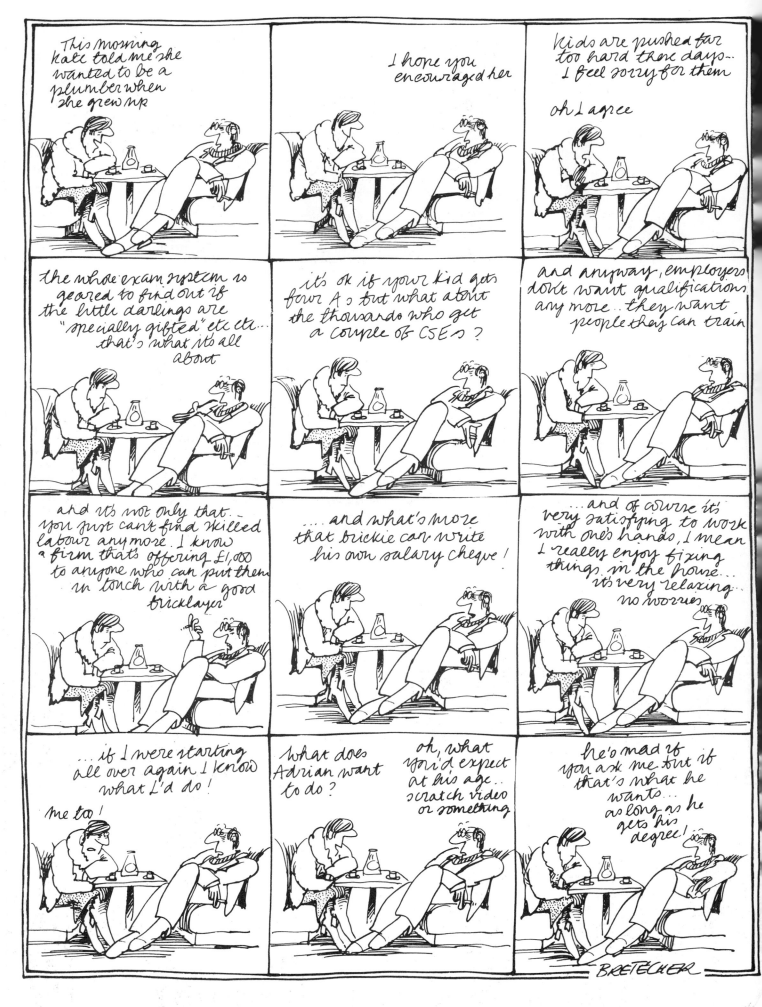

HAVE A JAR

BRETECHER

GRAPEVINE

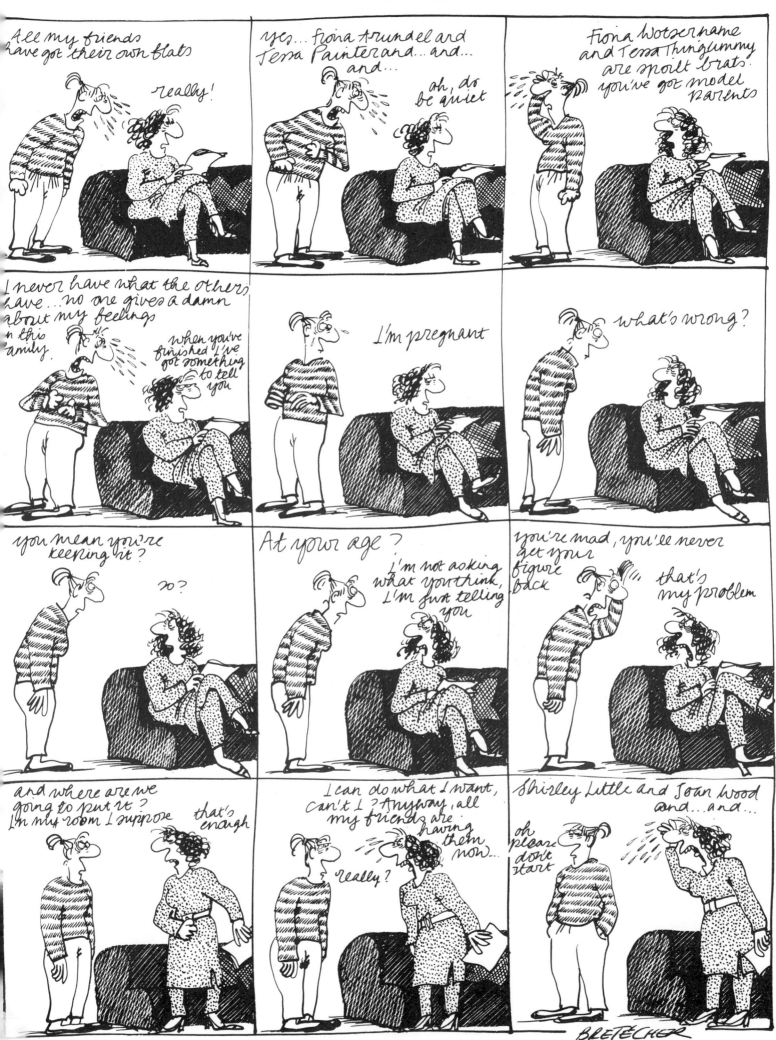

look what I just bought

it's one third charcoal, one third sawdust, one third wool... it eliminates 62% nicotine and 54% tar

oh, but have you seen this

it's a little plastic thing you stick on the end of your cigarette... it's transparent, you can hardly see it

it collects all the shit at the bottom... look I've only smoked two and it's already disgusting

after five cigarettes you just throw it away

they're all basically the same

when I unscrew mine... it's full of shit

yes, but yours isn't transparent

whereas mine lets you see all the tar building up you're genuinely aware of what you're inhaling

it's disgusting

look ... I'm only on my third and you can already see how.

see what I mean?

Christ!

and when you think you could have had all that in your lungs

when mine's full, I'd like to try yours

BRETECHER

68

I really like George

you can't blame him for what he's become... I've known him for twenty years

he had nothing to start with so he had to make up for a lot

I should know... I got him his first job... and it wasn't easy for him

they treated him like dirt... when management said "jump", he jumped

I often had to intervene and tell them all to lay off

and then George always had a thing about his looks... do you know why he's got that beard?

because he's got no chin... I mean really... it's a big problem for him

that time the firm banned beards, George got very depressed

and that didn't help his sex life of course... he lived like a monk for years

but that didn't stop him getting what he wanted... and if he's an arrogant and insensitive bastard he's got his reasons... why go into all that again

I suppose no matter what he does, I'll always have a lot of time for George

BRETÉCHER

MOTHER HENS